MANDALA

Poems by
Sam Hamill

Monotypes by
Galen Garwood

MANDALA

MILKWEED EDITIONS

MANDALA

Printed in the United States of America
Published in 1991 by Milkweed Editions

Milkweed Editions
528 Hennepin Avenue, Suite 505
Minneapolis, Minnesota 55403
Books may be ordered from the above address

ISBN 0-915943-52-2

94 93 92 91   4 3 2 1

Publication of this book is made possible in part by funding from The Bush Foundation, the Literature Program of the National Endowment for the Arts, the Star Tribune/Cowles Media Company, the Dayton Hudson Foundation for Dayton's and Target Stores, the First Bank System Foundation, the General Mills Foundation, the Jerome Foundation, the Minnesota State Arts Board through an appropriation by the Minnesota State Legislature, a McKnight Foundation Award administered by the Minnesota State Arts Board, the Andrew W. Mellon Foundation, the Northwest Area Foundation, and by the support of generous individuals.

Library of Congress Cataloging-in-Publication Data

Hamill, Sam.
    Mandala : poems / by Sam Hamill ; monotypes by Galen Garwood.
      p. cm.
    ISBN 0-915943-52-2 : $12.95
    I. Garwood, Galen.   II. Title.
  PS3558.A4235M36   1991
  811'.54 — dc20

91-3370
CIP

For Morris Graves
  and for Greg Mitchell, Tree Swenson, and Eron Hamill

Monotypes are single-state images produced by the manipulation of inks or paints on the clean surface of a printing plate. They are printed in a manner similar to etching, but unlike "edition" etchings, each print is unique even though the production of a monotype may include several passes through the printing press. Once a final image is achieved, the plate is wiped clean to be used again. The monotypes for *Mandala* were created by manipulating a series of templates and inks and solvents on an aluminum plate before each printing.

Acknowledgments:

The following originally appeared in *Ploughshares* (Vol. 17, No. 1, 1991): In the Beginning; The Gift of Tongues; Saigyo's Moon; Two Birds; Crossing the Great River; Lukianos.

The following were first published in *Blue Canyon Press* (Japan), 1990: The Gift of Tongues; Crossing the Great River; Alder Pollen; Returning.

"Malebolge: Prince William Sound" was first published in *Season of Dead Water* (edited by Helen Frost), Breitenbush Books, 1990.

"A Dragon in the Clouds" is reprinted from the book of that title published by Broken Moon Press, 1989.

"Saigyo Alone" is reprinted from *Only Companion*, translations from the Japanese, Shambhala Publications, 1991.

Only thought alone. Before the word, the image. Before the image, mind. Mind is only process; it is only beingness alone. Imagination strips away centuries of mere technique. The seer becomes the seen: the dance of Psyche, the joy of Moses, the humor in Bodhidharma's fierce, bushy brow.

In 1956, Carolyn Kizer presided over what Selden Rodman has described as an "artists' salon" in Seattle. She had written of a "renaissance in poetry" then underway, largely a consequence of the influence of Theodore Roethke and Stanley Kunitz. A large part of the inspiration for these poets (and not a few camp-followers) came from the paintings of the elder statesman Mark Tobey and from Morris Graves, who then lived in Edmunds, north of Seattle, in a house he designed and built himself. What the poets learned from the painters was a simple and profound lesson in elemental Zen: perfect technique, then abandon technique in order to surrender completely to inspiration. Technique is inevitably logical, it is the Confucian aspect of the painter's art; it insists upon perfect tone and perfect color; it imposes organization. Great art arises out of instinctive response to immediate, direct experience.

Mu Chi, painting his persimmons hundreds of years ago — in the *act* of painting — was not thinking about himself, Mu Chi, in the act of painting persimmons. Painting, he gave up self-awareness, entering a state of revelation wherein painter, ink, brush, and paper are one thing, the act revealing itself and in so doing, revealing something of the "personality" of Mu Chi. We would learn more from his image of persimmons than from a self-portrait, every self-portrait being a mask. Mu Chi is not concerned with technique. He is not concerned with personality. And yet his paintings offer evidence of an active intelligence, an inspired, engaged personality.

In thirty-five years, the Seattle Renaissance has been forgotten. The poetry of Carolyn Kizer, Theodore Roethke, and Stanley Kunitz endure like the work of Tobey and Graves. Why such a literary renaissance never came off can, in part, be explained by the reading at the Six Gallery in San Francisco in November of 1956, presided over by Kenneth Rexroth and featuring Allen Ginsberg, Gary Snyder, and friends, and the major literary renaissance which followed. Kizer's once-vital journal, *Poetry Northwest*, may have fallen beyond resuscitation. Washington currently ranks 46th in per capita spending on arts, spending less than half the national average. A community that refuses to support its artists can't expect them to remain and live on air and good intentions. Kizer moved on to become Director of the Literature Program at the National Endowment for the Arts. Tobey and Roethke are dead. Carl and Hilda Morris moved to Portland. Most of the Northwest School of painters became successful, either in the northwest or elsewhere. Kunitz and Graves moved on.

Despite a brief life, Kizer's little salon has exercised some influence among artists of all kinds in the Pacific Northwest, which is rooted in one shared idea: technique must be mastered and then, under inspired circumstances, be completely forgotten. To "think" in painting or verse or music is certain death to art. The real thinking arises naturally out of the act of composition itself. This latter form of thinking in art is usually referred to as "ideas." A painting or a poem is not *about* anything. It is only a measure, a sentence, the experience of light, a gesture leading into enlightenment.

The surest way to paint or write poorly is to sit down full of the idea of making a painting or a poem. There is a certain state akin to meditation in which poem or painting simply takes over, the artist being only an instrument in the expression of beingness, of elemental *thusness*. There is not exactly a beginning nor, exactly, an end. The discipline is timing.

Discipline. There was a time when a university student might be asked, "What is your discipline?" The word comes from the Old English *discipul* via the Latin *discipulus*, which derives from the earlier Latin *discere*, "to learn." As in, to *discern*. An artist learning his or her discipline becomes at some point a *disciple* of — usually — an elder artist.

But art is also an act of rebellion, existentially absurd perhaps, but as Graves himself has said, the outrageousness itself is neither good nor bad. Anyone familiar with the work of Tobey and Graves has entered the conversation (evidenced in paint) which transpires. It is not as simple as observing that Graves learned this or that valuable lesson in technique — the confluence of their respective disciplines served to broaden and deepen the awareness of each. But to state, as others have, that Graves used Tobey's "white writing" and returned it to "nature" through merely inserting the image of a bird is utterly sophomoric.

Morris Graves concentrates energy on making the *line*. In a Graves painting, the line functions visually in much the same manner as the *line* in Theodore Roethke's last and greatest poetry, the "North American Sequence" and "Meditations of an Old Woman," and others. The line becomes a *measure of revelation*. The other *materia mater* is of course as much a part of the construction — color, tone, rhyme, breath, and pulse. But the line is the basic unit. What came to be called "action painting" concerned itself with what happens when the line is transformed into something else. Graves's sonic broom loaded with ink.

Art criticism is to the painter as literary criticism is to the poet: the poet or painter is midwife, the critic is a coroner. Painters converse as much as poets, and nearly as much as musicians (who indeed revel in an alternately pejorative and ecstatic idiom). Their greatest conversations are recorded in non-verbal "essays" and gestures.

Kizer's gathering of poets, fueled by the rich imaginations of Kunitz and Roethke, may in fact have been a continuation or transformation of the conversation begun between Morris Graves and Guy Anderson in 1929. Graves, nineteen at the time, had seen Anderson's paintings at the Fifth Avenue Gallery. Anderson was only four years older, and the two formed a friendship bonded by the studio they came to share. The dialogue begun in their studio would grow in the Thirties to include George Tsutakawa, Kenneth Callahan, Fay Chong, Carl and Hilda Morris, and of course Tobey.

By 1940, Margaret Tomkins had joined the group, and they gathered frequently at Tobey's studio for stimulating explorations of the role of art and artist in society. In his essay on Guy Anderson, Bruce Guenther credits Tobey's Bahai faith for encouraging the group's "wide-ranging explorations of both Western and Eastern philosophies and religions." Anderson, however, had been raised in a house with Asian art, and Graves was already deeply interested in Zen. Later, Anderson and Tobey would discuss the similarities between Northwest Coast Native American art and bronzes of the Han and Shang dynasties.

Not much has been made of the fact that virtually all the members of what became called the Northwest School of painters were conscientious objectors. Being a conscientious objector in a society which has waged almost perpetual war for nearly three hundred years requires self-examination at the most penetrating level; it is a decision which shapes an entire life, a commitment which informs every act. Among the most startling of revelations resulting from profound introspection is that the most dangerous individual is the one who murders indirectly, through complicity, by insisting upon the right to remain ignorant — those who commit murder at the ballot box after communion.

In a 1958 painting, "Ant War," Graves explores the economics of war, black and red ants each protecting an identical hoard, each side prepared for total confrontation. Taken as a statement on the economics of the Cold War then raging, the painting has power and humor and not a little pathos. Twenty years earlier, before the official beginning of World War II, Graves had painted "English Nightfall," a tortured Queen Ann chair caught twisted in a web of indecision, a tear in the eye on the chairback, one clawed leg gripping another. French and Papal nightfalls soon followed. There were German and Italian and Russian nightfalls, visionary paintings of objects writhing and disintegrating. But as the world burst into war, Graves turned more and more deeply to nature, his images of birds taking on greater personality as in "Bird with Possessions" and "Bird in the Spirit," both from 1943.

Eventually, the Holocaust came to an end. On August 1, 1945, following weeks of firebombing Tokyo — at the rate of one bomb for every five square meters of the city — Hirohito attempted to surrender, but the U.S. deemed the surrender insufficiently unconditional. The Japanese wanted only to preserve the life of their emperor. A week later, Hiroshima and Nagasaki were bombed. The world entered a nuclear nightmare. And the Japanese surrendered with the condition that their emperor's life be spared. Europe and Japan began rebuilding. The Cold War began in earnest. Joseph McCarthy became the self-appointed thought patrol of the nation. Eisenhower, timid as ever, hid his eyes and ears and turned his head away. Truman called Ike "chickenshit" for not facing down the alcoholic, hate-mongering senator from Wisconsin.

And Morris Graves explored consciousness achieving the form of a crane. Eisenhower sent U.S. troops into Southeast Asia to "protect our investments in tin and tungsten." The civil rights movement was born with Rosa Parks sitting in the "White only" section of an Alabama bus in 1954. Rock-and-roll took over popular culture. And Jasper Johns became famous by painting American flags. Jackson Pollack dripped paint; Franz Kline and Ben Shahn painted bold, heavily calligraphic pieces; and Morris Graves continued to paint loons and hibernating animals and Buddhist and Shinto symbols, exploring the deepest part of consciousness where personality dissolves into mere suchness as we continue to spin our small blue planet into the infinite void. Fads and fashions in the art world came and vanished. Human joy and human misery remained elementally unchanged.

And as he continued to draw images inspired by the natural world, Graves drew more and more deeply from spiritual traditions of the East, especially Japanese Zen. The art of Morris Graves forms an almost continuous line leading directly into perfected silence. Informed that Jackson Pollock had not painted in two years, he replied, "That's all right, too!"

Shang bronzes, Buddhist mandalas, figures and ideas drawn from the early Greeks, hieratic Egyptian birds, Haida and Tlingit ceremonial carvings — it is all the work of the heart, the expression of Mind. Graves loads a broom with ink and gives a great WHACK! to a large sheet of paper. "Machine Age Noise." How long does it take to make such a painting? In this particular case, approximately forty thousand years, reckoning roughly from early cave paintings and petroglyphs. It is a *whack* informed by Zen calligraphy, koan, ritual, and visionary traditions. It is a *whack* of glee, a *whack* of revelation.

Art demolishes nationality, removing even the barrier of language to reveal the unfettered thusness of universal experience. Little understood, Graves has been variously identified as a kind of nature painter, an occultist, an eccentric personality recognizable mostly from a famous photograph by Imogen Cunningham taken in 1973, the monkish painter walking in his leek garden with a blanket over his shoulders. Graves, as much a citizen of Kamo no Chomei's mountains near Kyoto or of a Sung dynasty village as he is a citizen of the contemporary Pacific Northwest, seems far more interested in the highly refined calligraphic technique of ancient masters than with experimental abstractions going on all around him. While others defined and exhausted "action painting," he refined the ancient art of meditative painting. In the midst of the cacophonous twentieth century, he achieves silence.

Protective of his privacy in order to protect his meditation, Graves carries forward ideas and practices of the Ashikaga school of Japan, zen-infused visions drawn from early Ch'an, even Hindu, meditative practices, shamanistic visions not the least at odds with those of Haida and Tlingit or Hebrew mystic and consistent, eighty years later, with the integrated watershed of his birthplace in the Fox

Valley of Oregon in 1910. He is not so different from the famous fourth century Confucian recluse, T'ao Ch'ien. Like other visionaries, he remains isolated at the perimeter of the society whose very soul most needs him.

It is within this connection to inexhaustible spirit — freedom within tradition, technique completely mastered so as to be forgotten — that Morris Graves has prospered, rich in mutalaic vision, his paintings returning us to sanity in an age which glorifies and advocates the absurd notion that we can or should achieve immediate self-gratification. This futile obsession leads directly to the beginning of the end for Prince William Sound, the Persian Gulf, indeed for the entire planet.

Part of our cultural heritage includes the fundamental conviction that human rights are the primary resource of a nation, an idea articulated by our acknowledged forebears, a committee of slaveholders who conspired to commit genocide against Native American cultures across the entire continent. Perhaps because the element of hypocrisy existed at the birth of the nation, it has persisted in our social attitudes, including an unstated devotion to "manifest destiny" as it applies to personal wealth, regardless of whose cheap labor provides such wealth. Graves has addressed social identity through his quiet insistence upon a personal vision reflecting personal responsibility. Like any number of his contemporaries who also saw the beginning of the end reflected in our abuse of natural resources — the fencing of open land, the damming of rivers, over-population, the invention of The Bomb — Graves draws heavily on naturalism, but his fishes, birds, and animals most often bear a world-weary expression of ancient resignation. He has not been interested in hieratic emblems like those of Georgia O'Keeffe, nor in grand gestures like the New York painters who began "movements" in art. He has remained patient, at least one step removed from the commercial world of art, an artist more interested in process than in wealth, a seer somewhere alone down the long journey, alone and taking notes.

Galen Garwood and I first began discussing a collaborative homage to Morris Graves while still at work on our initial collaboration, *Passport* (Broken Moon Press, 1989). We decided to reverse our previous order and let the poems come first. With an opening lyric salutation, a kind of prolegomenon, I began exploring what I considered key images and attitudes I had admired in Graves's work through most of my life. The resulting images connected directly to certain "classic" ideas: the figures of Herakleitos and Lukianos, of T'ao Ch'ien and Lao Tzu, of Ekichu and Kawabata Yasunari making cameo appearances — often in dreams. There is a dialogue from Master Kung (Confucius) from the *Lun Yu;* John Milton's stern countenance; an impassioned warning sprung from a conversation between Dante and Ugolino in the Seventh Circle of Hell, where Dante places those who commit crimes against Nature.

Garwood, gathering the poems into a single canvas, manages to avoid "illustrating" the poems by concentrating his listening on their totality rather than on their particular images. His images "re-present" movement and stasis and the abstraction of "wisdom" born of traditional oral teachings. Just as I have not been interested in drawing my verse from literal readings of Graves' paintings, Garwood has chosen abstract over literal readings of my poems. He is no more interested in "interpreting" my poems than I am in interpreting Morris Graves' paintings. Each is a part of the whole, the wheel of the mandala spinning endlessly on.

Those early dialogues between Graves and Tobey, Graves and Anderson, Kizer, Roethke, and, later, the poet John Logan — those dialogues between visual and aural artists, between writers and painters and visionaries from diverse epochs and cultures — those dialogues carried forward from the 30s and 40s and 50s — continue. Their shadows and echoes resound throughout these pages.

My questions or meditations in lyric form are answered in Garwood's wealth of black-and-white. Now microscopic, now galactic, a little blank-faced bird watches from his images, sky swelling, floating away in its blank eyes, the days and nights beyond number. Its face, utterly expressionless, resembles a cassette tape from which the music of the spheres is played. If the poet suggests image through sound, the monotypist suggests sound through image. The apparent enigma completes the whole.

It has been our intention to work through a number of themes found in the art of Morris Graves, *not* to copy images from his paintings and drawings. In this, it has been our desire to articulate a mandala of which we are each a part. The articulation of a mandala forms a kind of sutra, a holy incantation. One way to write the word "poetry" in Chinese or Japanese is to combine the word *temple* with the word *word* — so the poem is both a temple built of words and words *of* a temple. The Chinese painter's brush-strokes are informed by the study of calligraphy. Studying the paintings of Morris Graves is like listening to a John Coltrane or Abdullah Ibrahim, it is a *going-to-churchness.* But Garwood and I enter not a vast cathedral but a small room of the mind, a room with tatami mats and with little pillows to sit on, the *zafu,* hoping we can sit until our buttocks rot like the Buddha's.

Morris Graves has been our inspiration, an inexact model, another living Buddha, another mandala *within which* we begin — Graves is a mandala upon which this mandala turns like the Great Wheel, and about which this mandala elaborates. Seer and seen are not two things. The tears and laughter of Moses are caught forever in Bodhidharma's big bushy beard. Palms together (*gassho!*), we come to Morris Graves to pay homage, to bow: at the beginning, at the end, word and image, thought and deed, are one.

— Sam Hamill

MANDALA

IN THE BEGINNING,
                    not The Word, but that which
precedes the word; not a word, but what
composes words — alfa and beta, a bull's horns
up-ended, perhaps authenticating the "ah"

of cognition: Memory — Mnemosyne
is mother of the Muses — memory
growing, tree-like: it is true the root
of *Tree* and *Truth* is *Dru*: the people

of the tree, Druids, also of the family
of memory which flowers, grows
perpetually widening concentric rings —
the single grain of sand dropped into the surf

extending its sphere of influence to the world's
farthest shores, an elemental image at core:
seeing the *daleth* in a *D*, the door
opening on the sea, hinged to swing wide,

revealing inscape — the great Unknown:
memory hung by core image
juxtaposed with outward countenance:
the "meaning" of words; the "skin
of the poem," the artlessness of art:

to evoke is to transform.

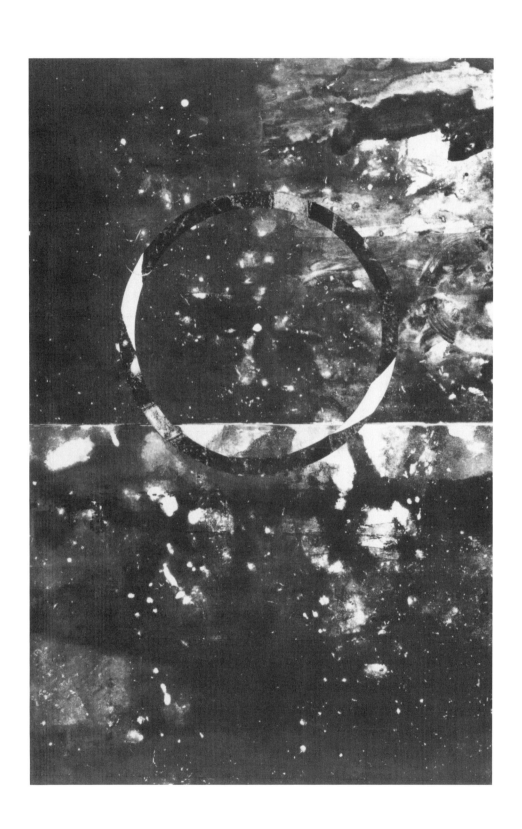

The Gift of Tongues

Everything I steal, I give away.
Once, in pines almost as tall as these,
same crescent moon sliding gently by,
I sat curled on my knees, smoking with a friend,
sipping tea, swapping Coyote tales and lies.

He said something to me
about words, that each is a name,
and that every name is God's. I who have
no god sat in the vast emptiness silent
as I could be. *A way that can be named*

is not the way. Each word reflects
the Spirit which can't be named. Each word
a gift, its value in exact proportion
to the spirit in which it is given.
Thus spoken, these words I give

by way of Lao Tzu's old Chinese, stolen
by a humble thief twenty-five centuries later.
The Word is only evidence of the real:
in the Hopi tongue, there is no whale;
and, in American English, no Fourth World.

Saigyo's Moon

I.

Looking everywhere,
there's no one around
to ease my gloom.
I'll make friends with the moon.

II.

This autumn moon
despises one
who clouds this sky
with teary eyes.

III.

What can one do? Sigh
heavily over the moon,
bathed in its beautiful light?
Tears, tears and sighs.

IV.

You stole my heart.
Now, alone, I watch
the wild goose fly north,
likewise alone and lonely.

V.

That moon in the sky
is our only souvenir.
If you see it, remember:
our hearts are always near.

VI.

A temple bell, night and day,
ringing pure and true
erases all illusions
but my dreams of you.

VII.

I wish you would come
with the moon every night,
stealing out to see me,
our shadows side by side.

VIII.

The whole cold night long
I held the old moon
in tear-soaked arms:
remembering our autumns.

IX.

Looking at the moon,
remembering words
spoken to only you:
how can my heart continue?

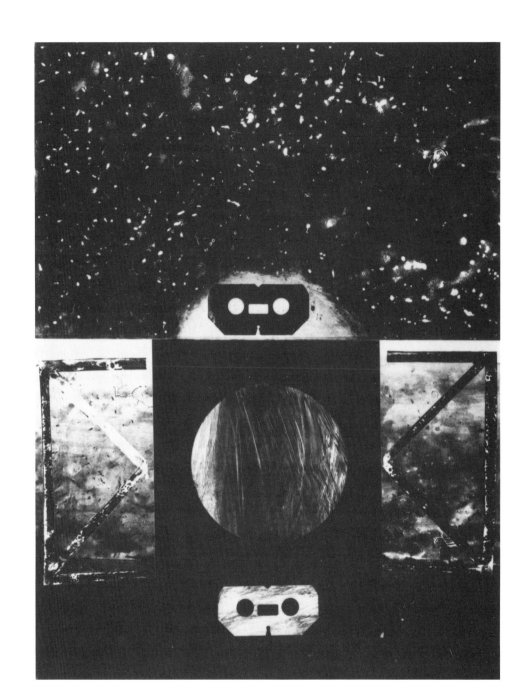

TWO BIRDS
               bound in friendship nest in a single tree.
One watches the world.
The other feeds on sweet fruit.

The Self, weary of pecking about, sinks into despair.
Through meditation, personal self comprehends impersonal self:
The Spirit soars!

When Sage and Spirit are united,
Lingam and yoni, good and evil
Vanish: they are one.

   .   .   .

Only in deepest meditation
Can Mind — grown utterly still —
Reveal the formlessness of truth.

The true self shines from the pure heart
When the five fires of living
Savage the mind.

(from the Mundaka Upanishad, Book Three)

Crossing the Great River

No one, Herakleitos said,
crosses the same river twice.
True enough. Every gain's
composed of losses.

Think, as Robert Duncan has,
of years as catches
where only that which one
loves well surpasses

our diurnal habit
of suffering and folly.
Years pass, crawling
into years. Too damned bad

for one who worships
childhood or youth. *Eyes,
dreams, lips, and the night passes.*
Every heart surprises.

The pale boatman won't hesitate:
he brings what night delivers:
the heart, flooding like a river,
and ourselves, bird-like, wading.

Lukianos

A weak man is like a broken jug:
although you pour in
     every kindness,
you pour in vain:
nothing is contained.

*   *

The vile mouth of the exorcist
     drives away demons,

not by virtue of his ritual,
     but by what his mouth excretes.

*   *

The poor painter captures
     only form, no other.

To find the voice
     you must trust color.

*   *

(from the *Greek Anthology*)

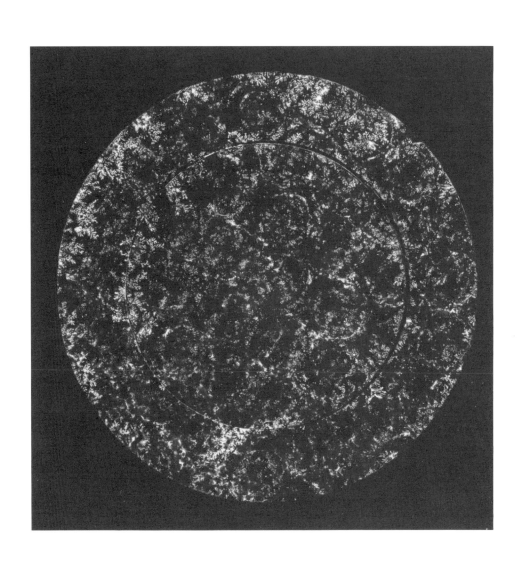

Painting True Nature

A man came to see Ekichu, 7th Master at Jufuku Temple and a famous painter. "Paint the fragrance of the famous line, 'After walking through flowers, the horse's hooves are fragrant,'" the man asked. Ekichu drew a butterfly fluttering near the hoof.

"Paint 'Spring breeze over the river bank,'" the man asked. Ekichu drew a bending willow branch.

The man recited a famous Zen couplet: "A finger points directly into the heart; see the Buddha-nature." He asked Ekichu to paint that heart, but Ekichu flung ink into the man's face, and when the man flushed with rage, Ekichu drew his angry face.

"Then paint the portrait of true nature," the man demanded.

Ekichu broke his brush in two. "There! If you haven't seeing eyes, you can't see it."

"Take another brush and paint the picture of true nature," the man demanded.

"Show me your own true nature and I'll paint that."

A Dragon in the Clouds

It is solstice —
hot, dry,
air too heavy to move,
the mountains hazy blue.

I have been baking in the sun
with Euripedes' fable of Helen.

And now, quietly,
a finch has flown down from the cedar
to perch on the window sill.

And I realize
she is curious,
she is watching,

and has cautiously stepped closer.

The beauty of the tragic,
the tragedy of the lovely,

she doesn't know or care to remember.

She knows two things:
the world is flat,
and that she lives

on this side
of the only river
she cannot fly across.

She looks at emeralds
in the grass and sees
only common seed.

And now she has come closer
once again,

her head cocked,
surveying my naked body.

Her eyes are large
and wearied by their knowledge,

like Kawabata's eyes
which knew
only sadness and beauty.

I close my book very slowly,
lay my head on my arms,
and look her in the eye:

she has become my lover
and my Dharma master.

Morris Graves says birds
inhabit a world without karma.

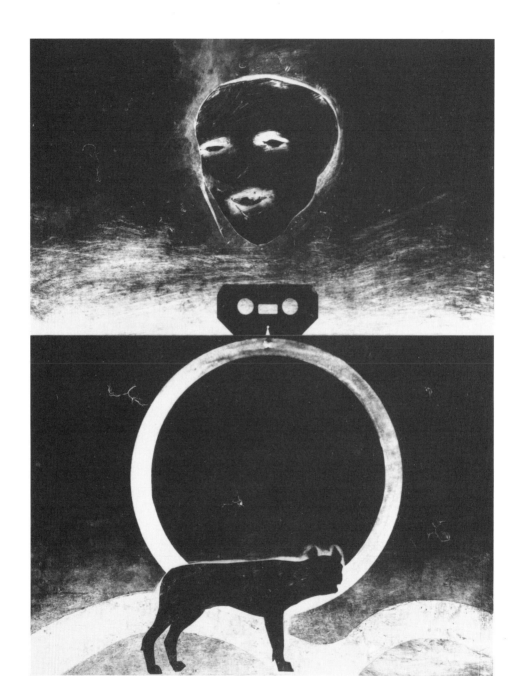

Night Bird

A bird then, but a bird
in moonlight filtered through
falling snow,

a small, delicate bird
of the soul, wide-eyed
at the whole wonderous world,

a tiny bird alone
within itself, yet *completed* somehow
only by moonlight and March snow,

a spirit-bird whose song
is utter silence,
who will not sing.

But not a painting.
Not even a sketch. Not a thing.
It is there, even now,

in the snows of the heart,
in the cold,
huddled in the night,

alone,
growing wise.

MASTER KUNG SAID: If one's motives are guided by profit, one creates ill will.

Master Kung said: One should not worry over having no official post; rather, worry whether you have qualifications. Do not brood over whether anyone appreciates your abilities; rather, be worthy of appreciation.

Master Kung said: A single thread binds my way.

Master Kung said: A great person understands what is moral; a small one, what is profitable.

Master Kung said: It is difficult to miss the mark while cleaving to essentials.

Master Kung said: Virtue does not stand alone; it has neighbors.

Master Kung said: My first students were rustics; the gentry followed later. In the use of music, I follow the former.

Mr. Chu went to see Master Kung, but the Master declined, claiming illness; as the messenger returned to Mr. Chu, the Master picked up his lute and sang, making certain Mr. Chu could hear.

(from the Lun Yu)

THE OLD MAN FROM WEST LAKE
                              set aside his long-handled hoe and sat down
in the shade under a broad tree, mopping his brow.
The sun moved toward mountains where a hawk was painted on the sky.

"There are some," he said, "who learn only the words.
You hear them running off at the mouth, fascinated
with their own useless eloquence,
their worthless cerebrations.
For them, every sentence is a victory.

"Many years ago, someone at the manor painted the outhouse
bright vermillion.
It served only to call more attention to the stench.

"Any damned fool can find a beginning.
The test of true character lies in bringing beginnings
to fruition."

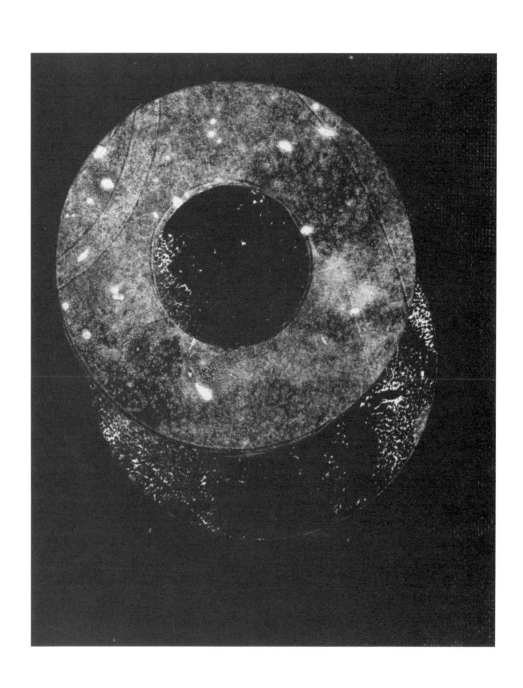

Lao Tzu called
                    for a grand return to Nature,
and he wandered, preaching *wu wei*.
Written music, he claimed, is artificial,
contrary to natural flow.

Mo Tzu demanded equal distribution of goods
and advocated universal love.
But music? "Music," he said,
"what a waste of time! It's counter-
productive, a great source of evil
in the world."

"All music," the Master said,
"is not *cheng sheng* — all music
is not wanton."

And the Master said, "The dance of Shao,
the eulogies of Wu,
this is music which puts mind and heart in order."

Having often enjoyed sitting under the Bo tree listening
as a plectrum danced among strings,
the Master closed his eyes as if listening
to echoes of the ages.

"There are those who know all the notes;
and there are those who know the music."

HORSES SCREAMED
                    in Picasso's "Guernica"
but no one heard, no one came.
Michael Spafford's "Labors of Hercules" draped
shames the flabby minds and bodies of The State.

New York galleries stuffed with choice
black-and-white two-dimensional graffito,
post-Holocaust nightmare urban vision —
hip rage, machine age noise.

Gauguin's melon-breasted native women
hum and laugh and sing.
Twilight casts a copper glow.
A lion, a monkey, and one bright moon.

Breughel's peasants abandon themselves
to dance. A small shadow
listens from a hill. The sky slants
away, blank as a raven's eye.

IMAGINE MILTON,
                almost blind,
composing a *Lycidas* or inventing a Paradise —
imagine Milton struggling to achieve
"the music of not overly excited speech."

There are and always have been
anarchists, avant-gardists, geeks
who would "liberate" Art
from the prisons of technique.

Blind Homer told his tale
as simply as he could.
Catullus cursed hypocrisy,
and if it stung, it should.

The Reverend Mr. Eliot
prepared his face to meet
the faces that you meet:
dry, courteous. So polite.

A single flower in a simple vase;
a sleeping owl, tired and wise;
a frond; a resilient young pine:
still life, still life, still life.

ALDER POLLEN. Daffodils. Clear, pale sky.
Clearing out underbrush and bucking wood,
I pause to wipe away my sweat, surprised
by this sudden deep stillness of the world.

In fifteen years, the underbrush has died,
choked by growing trees. Seedling evergreens
poke up through blackberry tangles — suffice
to say, they persevere. As if in a dream,

spring arrives, all of a moment. To die
on a day such as this might not be bad:
pale sky disappearing before my eyes,

a world unspeakably silent. I've had
all the best of it again. Chainsaw roar
as I pull the cord: white butterflies soar.

RETURNING

            from my journeys, I am amazed
to find new growth in cedar, spruce, and fir,
knobby alder turning gray as it ages,
as I turn gray. This land slowly regains
maturity, although it will never
reach climax again. I, somehow sustained
by the natural recovery of scarred land,
step certainly, one day nearer the grave.

If I miss my child, she grew wings and has flown.
This gorgeous blue sky can't possibly hide
the emptiness at its core. Growing
accustomed to the void, I nonetheless try
to make something of each brief day — a bead
of sweat, a breath — daybreak bursting like a seed.

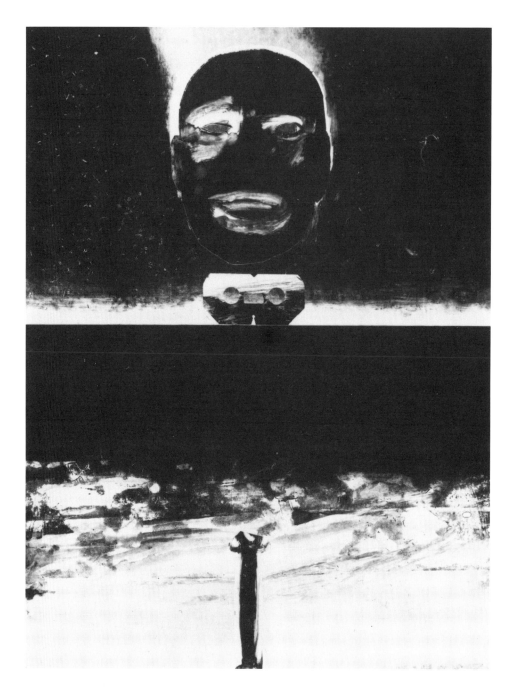

Arse Poetica

You stand like a twin-headed bird,
one head open-mouthed in song,
the other stitched tight in sorrow.
An odd dance of *yin* and *yang*.

You simply cannot escape
your own original face.
The Greeks called this
excessive ego *hubris*,

the consequence of the sin
being violence brought down
upon one's own fragile being:
karma: pride's other twin.

Charmed, the storyteller
is always surprised
by the hard truths
of his own enchanting lies.

As one perhaps might come
to Literature — capital L —
only to find — what in hell? —
Geoffrey Chaucer's bare red bum.

IO NO PIANGEVA;
                    si dentro impietrai.
Piangevan *elli* —

Dante's Ugolino,
recounting his suffering.

Because he could not wail,
he turned to stone inside.

Seferis on the riverbank
wanted only to speak simply,

"to be granted that grace."
Three hundred thousand tons

of non-biodegradable DDT
delivered into the watershed.

What we have done
cannot be undone.

Our silence turns
every heart to stone,

our ability to speak simply
lost, disgraced

by lies and misplaced
loyalties to false wealth

disguised
by more private and official lies.

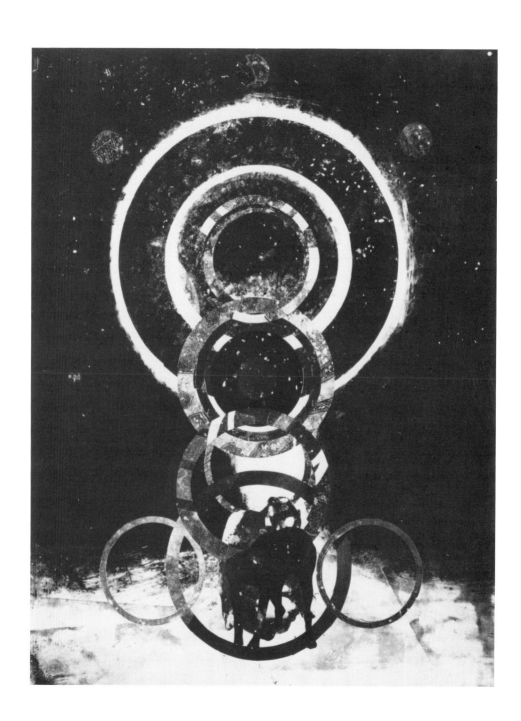

Malebolge: Prince William Sound

"This world knows them as a blind people,
    greedy, invidious, and arrogant;
cleanse yourself of their foul ways."

                  — Ser Brunetto Latini

to Dante,
        in the bowels of Hell's seventh circle,
and he named them: *gent' è avera, invidiosa e superba.*

And Brunetto said, "Know that I keep company
with clerics and with the literati
and with those who know grand fame,
and for each, the sin against earth is the same."

And going deeper, Virgil used Dante's belt
to summon Geryon from the depths,
to carry them on his back to the edge of Malebolge
where flatterers are immersed in excrement.

Teals. Terns. Eagle and raven. Sea otter, clam, and salmon.
The world's tallest mountains
are all under water. Porcupine, beaver, muskrat.
Brown bear and black bear and tiny brown bat.

The people of the soil — call us *human* anyway —
linger at the shore. We are only humus.
Bear and otter no longer out-swim us.
Loon, hawk, and wild goose no longer fly away.

Opening the heart's own book,
look! there's Dante in a man-made Hell,

entering Malebolge on the back of the beast he dreamed,
there are rivers of blood and misery;

there's old blind Homer
listening as tales of Odysseus wind and unfold;
there are tales of Tlingit and Haida and Kwakiutl;
the dance of Krishna, eighth avatar of Vishnu.

But nothing prepares the blood to assume
this speechlessness, profound silence of complete grief,
this vision of hell we can't escape
unfolding before our eyes.

Strangling on our own greedy, greasy lies,
the thick black blood of the ancient world
covers and clogs our lives.
What can be washed away is washed away

like history, tar-balls riding out the tides.
We turn back to our own anthropomorphic needs,
our creature comforts, our poems and our famous lies,
closing the book on Homer, Dante, and Brunetti,

closing the book of the heart
on the face of god, and on her counterpart:
rock, fish, bird, plant, and beast:
on you, on me, and on the Geryon we ride: Exxon Valdez.

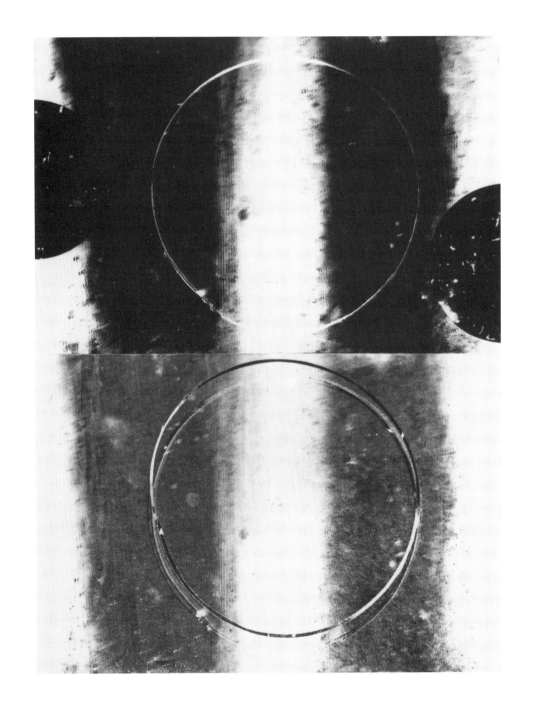

THINKING, READING LATE,
                              Denise Levertov's "Modulations for Solo Voice"
at the dead end of night, remembering Robert Duncan's great poem,

"My Mother would be a Falconress," hunting back over
                              that same fertile ground — "groundwork"
as in Duncan's own grand testimonial —
seeking the various threads of a fabric the way a painter might study
the fragile elegance of Asian handmade paper,
eye alert to subtle inconstancies, studying the material to become the material:
the lonely soul the only empty canvas the human heart must fill.

It is like loving an Anton Chekhov, an Akhmatova, a Su Tung-p'o —
the love is there and real, a tangible in this brief, intangible
                              world. Thus, the voice, enthralled, has no choice but to speak.
Lu Chi dips his brush because he must.

May a poet write *amor?* Was there ever a mother who did
                              not hum? Art is not *for.*
Art is mother of the soul, but no romantic vision can dissuade the heart's own
existential leanings. The heart rises like a bird of prey and then returns,
humbled, to its hood. Rice paper. Mulberry paper. A voice like gouache.

Moonset. It is all one thing. I have stayed up so late,
I might as well stay up. The voice, like the heart, modulates.
It grows light.

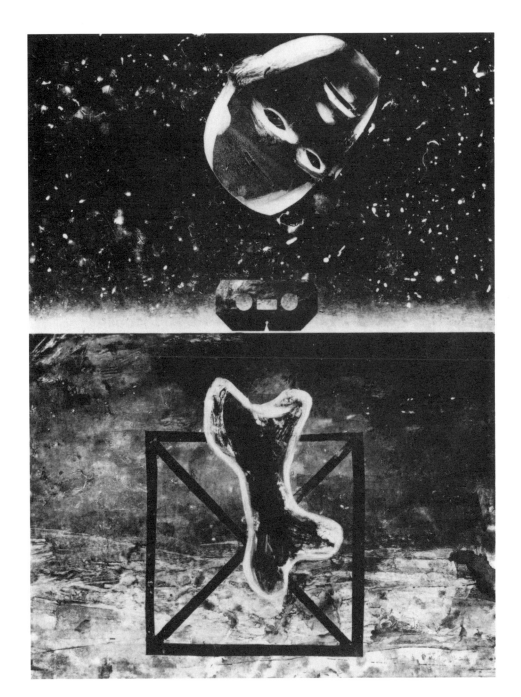

Old Dragon Bone

I found a bird's leg —
or maybe an old dragon bone —
small, almost weightless,
a phantom bone, a mystery.
You could trace it back
to a huge pterodactyl,
down through the Great Bird
which rose out of its ashes,
through moon-bird, sun-bird,
and bird-of-the-morning star.
A distant descendant,
this clean white bone is common —
slight, fragile, almost
like a feather in the hand.
A faint song too sweet
to last long, this dragon bone's
an ordinary
robin, sparrow, or starling.
Listen hard for the wingbeat.

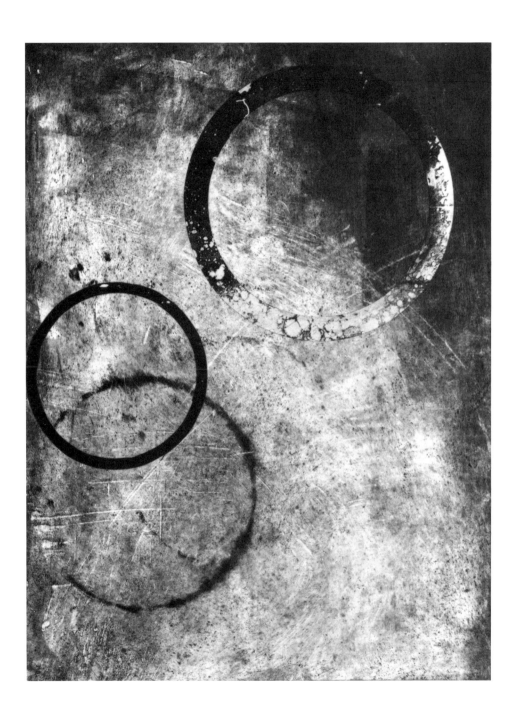

Li T'ai-po's Fall River Song

On Old River Mountain
a huge boulder swept clean
by the blue winds of heaven
where they have written
in an alphabet of moss
an ancient song.

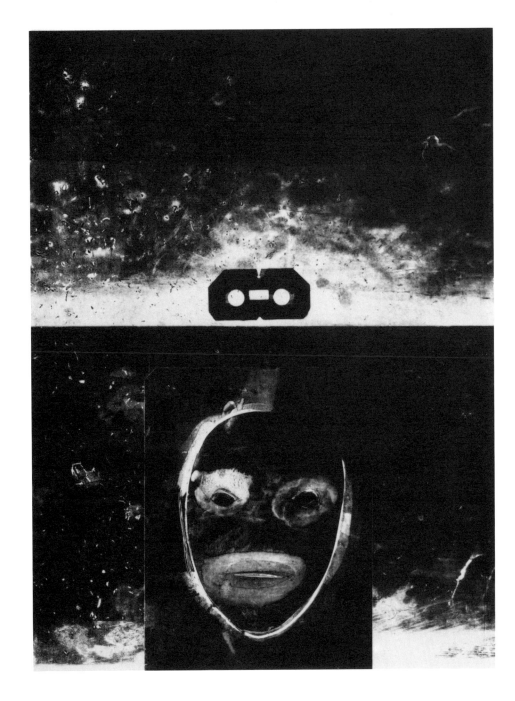

Two Faces of T'ao Ch'ien

To Cousin Ching-yuan
  Twelfth Month, 403

Hidden behind a rustic gate,
I sever my ties with the world.

Some days I look, but no one's there,
the old wooden gate stays closed.

Cold, the cold year-end winds,
snows cloaking everything.

Bending my ear, I hear nothing.
My eyes hurt from white light,

winter air sharp as a blade up my sleeve.
Rice bowl and wine jug empty,

in the whole desolate house
there is nothing to sustain me.

Reading the classics again,
sometimes I still find heroes,

old sages I dare not emulate,
but who stood strong in adversity.

I've mastered the art of poverty.
I didn't come here seeking fame.

My meaning lies beyond my words —
who but you can understand my fate?

Passing through Ch'ien-hsi
  Third Month, 405

Months and years have flown
since I last traveled these hillside streams.

From dawn to dark I watch:
not a thing has changed.

Soft rain washes the trees,
bird on rising breeze —

all things self-revealing,
all things interlinking.

Is this where I belong,
pressed to meet my duties?

My body may be subject
but my heart remains my own.

I dream all day of fields and meadows,
and long all day to return.

Lost, I long for a boat back home.
The cypress survives the frost.

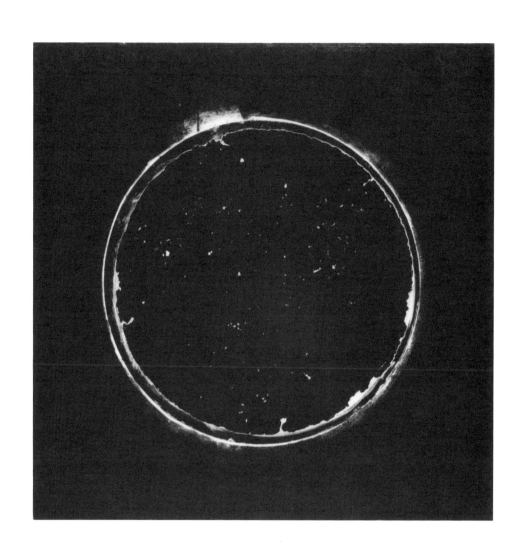

Saigyo Alone

No one visits me
this long way from the city.
All alone at last,
caged in this crack in the rock,
I give myself to grieving.

———

The mind is all sky,
the heart utterly empty,
and the perfect moon
is completely transparent
entering western mountains.

To a Difficult Friend

I see you've come up with
one of those old discarded masks
I used to wear.

Even at this distance, looking
in through the empty black eye-holes
I can almost see you

crouching in the dark,
alone and breathing hard. I didn't
mean to frighten you, I swear.

Having gone a long time without
seeing its cold exterior resemblance,
I mistook it

for a human face and spoke,
therefore, straight, almost nakedly.
I should apologize,

and do. And offer you
this song or poem as a token
behind which

I too may hide,
unutterably human,
almost, almost alive.

Masks

A Mask for Janus

Removing the mask to reveal the mask:
sadness in the twigs of the swan's nest.

Blind Justice

Abstract weight and measure, eternal brevity of years:
poised, impassive, she watches with her ears.

The Dance of Shiva

Thunder in the heartbeat:
breath drawn up through the feet.

Codependent Origination

Consciousness, without loss or gain,
achieves the form of a crane.

Contra Naturam

In complete discord with nature, we stand poised
above the eternal abyss of machine age noise.

Your Own Original Face

Before your parents were born,
it was everything you owned.

Samsara

"Experience" measures the movement of mind:
what we bring with us we leave behind.

Death Mask

Removing the mask at last,
you reveal another mask.

Galen Garwood was born in 1944 in Blakely, Georgia, and educated at the University of Alaska and the University of Washington. His monotypes, paintings, and collages have been given solo exhibitions at the Gerard Gallery in Toronto, Foster-White Gallery in Seattle, the Tacoma Art Museum, and in galleries from Gainesville, Florida, to Santa Monica, California. He has been included in international group exhibitions including *La Passion de Dunkerque* (Paris, Dunkerque, Taiwan) and *Galerie Imperatif Present* (Toulouse, France), the Musee des Beaux-Arts de Carcassonne, Musee des Beaux-Arts de Pau, and many others. His awards include first place in painting in the Pacific Northwest Annual, an exhibitors award from the American Academy of Arts and Letters, and a Washington Governor's Award for his previous collaboration with Sam Hamill (*Passport,* 1989).

Sam Hamill was born in 1942, probably somewhere in northern California, abandoned during World War II, and grew up on a ranch in Utah. He is the author of more than two dozen books, including ten volumes of original poetry, translations from classical Chinese, Japanese, Greek, Latin, and Estonian, and three volumes of essays. He has been the recipient of fellowships from the Guggenheim Foundation, the National Endowment for the Arts, and the Japan-U.S. Friendship Commission. Recent books include *A Poet's Work: the other side of poetry* (essays), the 3rd century Chinese *Art of Writing* by Lu Chi, a new translation of Matsuo Basho's *Narrow Road to the Interior*, and an anthology of Japanese tanka, *Only Companion*. He has been editor at Copper Canyon Press for twenty years and, like Galen Garwood, lives along the Strait of Juan de Fuca near Port Townsend, Washington.

designed by R.W. Scholes
body type 12/15 Perpetua
set by Graphic Arts Services
printed by Gopher Printing
on Mohawk Superfine acid-free paper